DISCARD

COUNTRIES  OF THE WORLD

AUSTRALIA

Andrew Kelly

with photographs by David Bowden

Illustrated by Malcolm Walker

The Bookwright Press
New York · 1989

Titles in this series

Australia

Canada

France

Great Britain

New Zealand

The United States

West Germany

Cover *Sydney Harbor Bridge and the Opera House.*

Opposite *Ayers Rock, or Uluru, is a sacred Aboriginal place. It was returned to the Aborigines in 1983.*

First published in the
United States in 1989 by
The Bookwright Press
387 Park Avenue South
New York, NY 10016

First published in 1988 by
Wayland (Publishers) Ltd
61 Western Road, Hove
East Sussex BN3 1JD, England

© Copyright 1988 Wayland (Publishers) Ltd

Library of Congress Cataloging-in-Publication Data
Kelly, Andrew
    Australia / by Andrew Kelly
        p.   cm.
    Bibliography: p.
    Includes index.
    Summary: Discusses Australia's history, culture,
family life, education, religion, and government.
    ISBN 0-531-18184-7
    [1. Australia — Juvenile literature. 2. Australia.]
I. Title.
DU96.K45 1988
994 — dc 19   87-34112
                                                       CIP
                                                        AC

Typeset by Oliver·Dawkins Ltd. Burgess Hill, West Sussex.
Printed in Italy by G. Canale and C.S.p.A.

Contents

All words that appear in **bold** in the text are explained in the glossary on page 46.

1 Introducing Australia

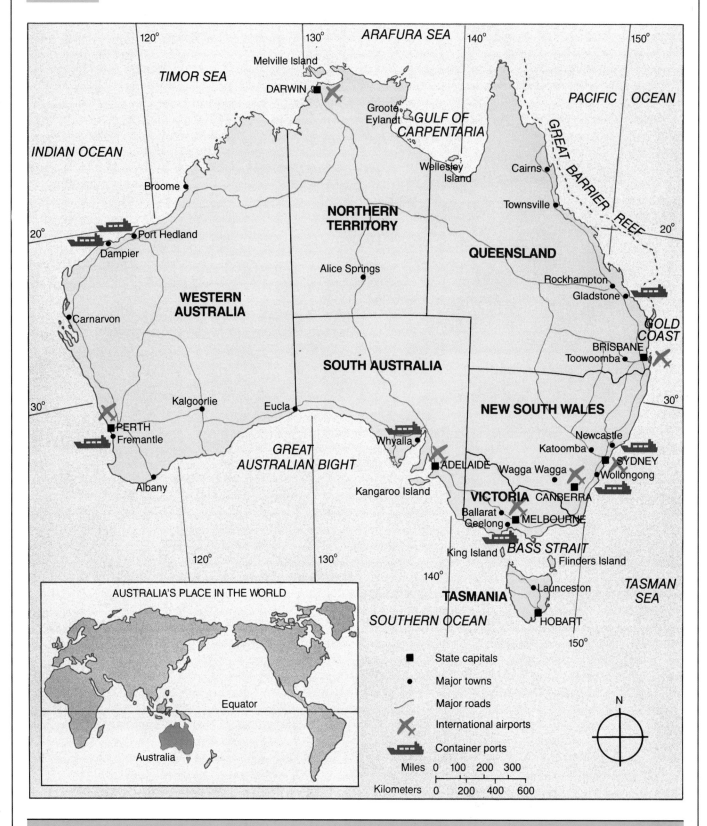

AUSTRALIA'S PLACE IN THE WORLD

Equator

Australia

■ State capitals

● Major towns

Major roads

✕ International airports

🚢 Container ports

Miles 0 100 200 300

Kilometers 0 200 400 600

Map labels:

ARAFURA SEA

TIMOR SEA

Melville Island

DARWIN

Groote Eylandt

GULF OF CARPENTARIA

Wellesley Island

PACIFIC OCEAN

GREAT BARRIER REEF

INDIAN OCEAN

Broome

NORTHERN TERRITORY

Cairns

Townsville

QUEENSLAND

Port Hedland

Dampier

Alice Springs

Rockhampton

Gladstone

WESTERN AUSTRALIA

Carnarvon

GOLD COAST

BRISBANE

Toowoomba

SOUTH AUSTRALIA

Kalgoorlie

Eucla

NEW SOUTH WALES

Newcastle

Katoomba

PERTH

Fremantle

Whyalla

GREAT AUSTRALIAN BIGHT

ADELAIDE

Wagga Wagga

SYDNEY

Wollongong

Albany

Kangaroo Island

CANBERRA

VICTORIA

Ballarat

Geelong

MELBOURNE

King Island

BASS STRAIT

Flinders Island

Launceston

TASMAN SEA

TASMANIA

SOUTHERN OCEAN

HOBART

Australia, along with the island state of Tasmania, is the world's largest island and the smallest **continent**. It is a land mass of 7,682,300 sq km (2,966,136 sq mi). This makes it as large as the continental United States. It has a population of about 16 million, which means it is very sparsely populated. There is an average of only two people per sq km (.39 per sq mi).

Australia is located in the **Southern Hemisphere** between the Indian and the Pacific Oceans. Tasmania, 67,800 sq km (26,178 sq mi), is off the southeastern coast. Sydney, on the east coast, is about as far south of the **equator** as Los Angeles, California, is north of it. About one-third of the country lies within the **tropics** and much of it is desert; yet on the mountains in the southeast, snow falls in winter. Most people live in the **temperate** parts of the country.

Throughout its history — long before the coming of the first **Aborigine** — Australia has been isolated from the rest of the world by the surrounding seas. This has meant that plants and animals have **evolved** in isolation, and many species can be found only in Australia.

An Australian Sikh family in New South Wales.

Aborigines, the first inhabitants of Australia, came from the north by raft or boat. For many thousands of years they had little contact with other cultures. Australia was the last large land mass to remain unknown to Europeans, and they did not settle there until 1788.

Australia's closest cultural links are with Britain and Western Europe, although, geographically, it is much closer to Asia, especially the islands of Southeast Asia. Many Australians are **immigrants**. In the past, most immigrants came from Europe, but today more come from Asia.

Left These red kangaroos are using their tails to prop themselves up and are boxing with their forepaws.

2 Land and climate

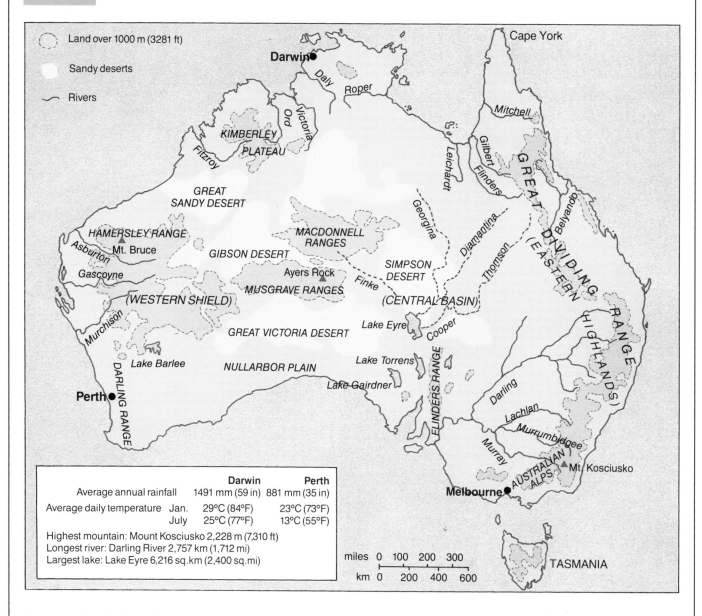

Land over 1000 m (3281 ft)

Sandy deserts

Rivers

	Darwin	Perth
Average annual rainfall	1491 mm (59 in)	881 mm (35 in)
Average daily temperature Jan.	29°C (84°F)	23°C (73°F)
July	25°C (77°F)	13°C (55°F)

Highest mountain: Mount Kosciusko 2,228 m (7,310 ft)
Longest river: Darling River 2,757 km (1,712 mi)
Largest lake: Lake Eyre 6,216 sq.km (2,400 sq.mi)

miles 0 100 200 300
km 0 200 400 600

Australia is the flattest, the driest and the smallest of the continents. The highest mountain, Mt. Kosciusko, is only 2,228 m (7,310 ft). Australia is flat because there have been no recent (in geological terms) episodes of **mountain building**. The land has gradually been eroded away by the forces of wind, rain and sun over millions of years.

The continent can be divided into three parts. The highest part of the country, called the Eastern Highlands, runs along the eastern rim of the continent, from Cape York in the north to Melbourne in the south. The other two parts are the Central Basin and the Western Shield. The Western Shield is a vast **plateau** of ancient rock. It is the oldest part of the country. Some of its rocks are billions of years old and are among the oldest rocks known. It is in the Shield that most of Australia's rich mineral deposits are found. The Central Basin used to be flooded by ancient seas and now there are a number of massive seasonal lakes, such as Lake Eyre, which fill only during very wet seasons.

Much of Australia is very dry. The average rainfall is only 465 mm (18 in), though rainfall varies from less than 150 mm (6 in) in the central deserts to more than 2,000 mm (78 in) in isolated pockets in the tropical north and in the ranges of Tasmania. Much of the land is desert or semidesert. It is rain, or rather the lack of it, that determines where people live and how the land is used. Most people choose to live on the coast, where the rainfall is greatest.

Above *Australia is the driest of continents and droughts are common.*

Below *The Olgas are a group of strange rounded domes of sandstone in Central Australia.*

3 Australian environments

Much of Australia is desert. Because it is so dry and little can grow, the heart of the continent is called the "Dead Center." Toward the coast the vegetation increases as the rainfall increases. From desert you might pass from grassland to **savannah** and then into woodlands, which Australians call *mallee* or *mulga*. Then the trees gradually become thicker and taller until, near the coast, there is true forest.

Although much of the country is dry, some small pockets of Australia are so wet that **rain forests** grow. Most of the Australian rain forests are in Queensland. Rain forests are very rich and varied environments. They are also very fragile environments because the rain washes much of the plant foods out of the soil. The Australian rain forest is of great scientific interest, as it contains many primitive plants. North Queensland rain forests have been called "the cradle of the flowering plants." Above the snowline, where it is too cold for trees to grow in the winter, there are the **alpine** meadows. Rare and beautiful plants also grow here. In the spring the wild flowers come out in a blaze of color.

Above top Sturt's desert pea. This plant grows in the dry parts of southern Australia and it is the floral emblem of South Australia.

Right Australian rain forests are only a small fraction of the world's rain forests.

Above Snowy River in Kosciusko National Park.

Right People protesting in Sydney against the destruction of Australia's rain forests in the Daintree region of North Queensland.

Australia is only sparsely populated, which has meant that many of its environments have been left undisturbed. With the growth of mining, the expansion of logging and of clearing for development, many environments are now endangered. A balance has to be struck between development and **conservation**.

4 Wildlife

Australian plants, animals and birds are unique because the continent has been isolated for so long. To the early scientists and explorers Australia was a strange country: the gum trees kept their leaves and lost their bark; the swans were black; and there were animals with the beaks of ducks that laid eggs (platypuses). When descriptions were sent back to Europe many people thought they were untrue.

Australia is rich in plant species — there are over 12,000. Most Australian trees are **hardwoods**. The most commonly found trees are **eucalyptus trees** and **wattles**. Eucalyptus, such as the gum tree, range in size from dwarf species to the largest hardwood in the world — the mountain ash. They grow in climates ranging from desert to alpine. Wattles are acacias related to the mimosas of Europe and North America.

Left The small yellow flower of the wattle tree.

Below Many early European settlers were surprised to discover that swans in Australia were black, not white like those in Europe.

Above The mouse-sized pygmy possum is a marsupial — it has a pouch in which it carries its young.

Most Australian mammals are marsupials — the female has a pouch in which she carries her young. In other parts of the world most marsupials died out thousands of years ago, but in Australia they were protected by the surrounding sea. The kangaroo is perhaps the best known of the marsupials. Other marsupials include the koala, the wombat, the marsupial mole and the Tasmanian devil.

Australia has over 600 species of birds. Parrots form one of the largest groups. These are often spectacularly colored and include perhaps the best-known Australian birds — the budgerigar, the cockatoo and the galah.

Since the first Europeans settled in Australia, a number of species of birds, animals and plants have become **extinct**. This has been partly due to the destruction of their **habitat**, hunting, and the introduction of cats and dogs into the environment. Steps have been taken to protect wildlife but some species are still on the verge of extinction.

Above The hairy-nosed wombat sleeps underground in the heat of day, emerging only at night to forage for food. Although it looks slow it is very alert and can run up to 40 km (25 mi) an hour over short distances if disturbed.

Left The large, flightless emu is common throughout inland Australia.

5 History: the Aborigines

There were perhaps as many as 750,000 Aborigines living in Australia when the first Europeans settled at Sydney Cove in 1788. They lived in several hundred separate tribes. Each tribe had its own language, beliefs, culture and territory.

Left Caves throughout Australia are galleries of Aboriginal painting.

Below A guide explains Aboriginal culture to tourists at an archaeological site in New South Wales.

Archaeologists believe that the Aborigines came from Southeast Asia many thousands of years ago — perhaps as long as 50,000 or even 100,000 years ago. The oldest archaeological discovery, some stone tools found on the bank of the upper Swan River near Perth, have been dated to 38,000 years ago. The skeleton of a man who lived 30,000 years ago has been found at Lake Mungo in New South Wales. Many other ancient Aboriginal sites have been discovered and archaeologists continue to find more. They are gradually building up a picture of the past and learning how human beings developed.

Aborigines were hunter-gatherers who used their knowledge of the land to gather food and to hunt animals. The women gathered roots, berries and seeds and hunted small animals. This provided more than half of the Aboriginal diet. The men hunted larger animals. These were a less certain source of food but they were highly prized. The Aborigines lived in balance with their environment and did not overuse it, so food was usually fairly plentiful.

They made tools from materials they could gather locally. They made sharp edges for cutting by chipping stone.

The Aborigines led a rich spiritual, emotional and artistic life. In their religions they worshiped the land and their ancestors. Today, many Aborigines choose to continue to live in the traditional manner, though the majority live in towns and cities.

Aboriginal carvings marking a grave site in New South Wales.

6 History:European settlement

Left *An illustration of Government House in Sydney, which opened for the first time in 1843.*

Below *British convicts sent to a penal settlement in Port Arthur, Tasmania, in 1830.*

Europeans had long believed that there was a vast land in the south that balanced the large land masses in the Northern Hemisphere. In the seventeenth century, a number of Dutch explorers landed on the north and west coasts of the land that they called New Holland. In 1770 Captain James Cook landed on the eastern coast and claimed it for England. The Aborigines, who had already been living there for thousands of years, considered it their own.

In 1788, eighteen years after Cook landed in Botany Bay, settlers arrived to establish the **colony** of New South Wales. Most of these first settlers were convicts. The prisons in Britain were overcrowded, so the government sent convicts to the newly discovered continent to begin a colony.

Gradually the colony established itself, and free settlers began to arrive. They began to move out from Sydney, the site of the first settlement, and establish sheep runs in **the bush**. This led to bitterness and conflict between the settlers and the Aborigines, as this was land on which the Aborigines lived and depended for their livelihood.

Other colonies were established by the British government elsewhere in Australia. In 1803 a penal colony was set up in Van Diemen's Land (now Tasmania). Then in 1809 the colony of South Australia was begun, though no convicts were sent there. Colonies in Victoria, Queensland and Western Australia followed.

As the colonies grew and developed, they gained self-government and established parliaments of their own. The last colony to get self-government was Western Australia in 1870. The continent of Australia was now a number of separate colonies with many interests in common. In 1901 they joined together in a **federation** of states, which they called the Commonwealth of Australia.

An original photograph of the opening of the Federal Parliament procession in Melbourne in 1901.

Important dates

50,000 B.C.	The approximate date of the arrival of the Aborigines in Australia from Southeast Asia.
A.D. 1606	The first European, a Dutchman named William Jansz, sights Australia.
1642	The Dutch explorer Abel Tasman lands in Tasmania.
1770	Captain James Cook lands in Botany Bay on the eastern coast of Australia and claims it for Britain.
1788	The First Fleet arrives at Sydney Cove under Captain Arthur Phillip to establish the first settlement in Australia — a penal colony.
1803	Matthew Flinders completes the first voyage around Australia in the *Investigator.*
1901	The Commonwealth of Australia (a federation of the states of New South Wales, Victoria, Tasmania, Queensland, Western Australia and South Australia) comes into being.
1914-18	World War I. Australia experiences its first major losses in a war in 1915 on the Gallipoli peninsula in Turkey.
1939-45	World War II. The Japanese bomb Darwin in 1942.
1975	The Liberal Party under Malcolm Fraser comes to power.
1983	The Fraser government is defeated in the election and the Australian Labour Party under Bob Hawke forms a government.
1988	Australia celebrates its Bicentennial — 200 years since the first European settlement.

7 The Australian people

Most Australians are immigrants or the descendants of immigrants. Only about one in a hundred people is an Aborigine. The First Fleet, which arrived in Sydney Cove in 1788 to begin the European settlement of Australia, had on board convicts from England, Ireland and Scotland. This pattern of immigration was continued for the next 150 years, and most immigrants, with notable exceptions such as the Chinese who came to work in the goldfields, were of British origin.

A Greek christening in Melbourne. Melbourne has the third largest Greek population of any city.

For 150 years Australian society was modeled along British lines and many people spoke of Britain as home, though they were born in Australia and had never visited Britain. After World War II (1939-45), however, much of this changed and many immigrants arrived in Australia from countries other than Britain. The immigrants included many **refugees** who had been displaced by the war. The "new Australians," as the postwar immigrants were called, came from many different countries. The largest group of non-British immigrants came from Italy and the next largest group came from Greece.

Australia is made up of many different cultures, religions and nationalities.

The "new Australians" have had an enormous impact on Australian society. Between 1945 and 1985 the population has more than doubled. One in four of Australia's present population was born overseas. The immigrants have brought with them their languages, their cultures and their cooking, all of which have added to and enriched the Australian way of life.

Immigrants from a particular place or country often tend to remain together in a certain **suburb**, town or city. Melbourne is the third largest city of Greeks in the world, after Athens and Thessaloniki. In recent years many of the immigrants have come from Vietnam; some of these were refugees.

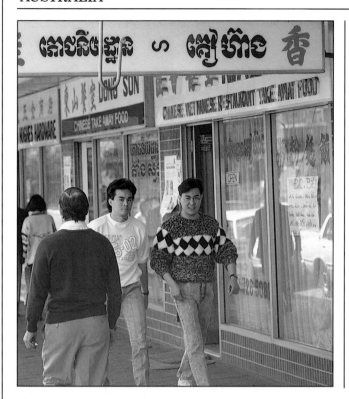

Most Australians think of themselves as strong, silent but friendly people. They think of themselves as people of the bush and of the countryside: a nation of **stockmen** and farmers, whose values have been shaped by a struggle with the environment. In Australia it is important to be "mates." Mates help each other out; they have a strong bond of friendship. Such a bond was needed in the bush, where people struggled against drought, bushfire and many other obstacles to survival.

Left Many Asians have come to live and set up businesses in Australia.

Below Bondi Beach is an extremely popular place for Australians to swim and surf.

The warm climate enjoyed by Australians means they can have barbecues outdoors whenever they wish.

This is at least how some Australians think. However, the reality is more complicated. Today, most Australians live in cities, and the typical Australian is as likely to be a Vietnamese chef, a Greek builder or a German doctor as a stockman from a cattle station in northern Queensland.

Australians prize the things they think make them "Australian." One thing a visitor would notice on arriving in the country is the accent. It does not, as in the United States, vary from place to place. People sound much the same from one side of the continent to the other, despite the vast distances crossed. This is true of many other things as well — the Australian lifestyle, for example, is very similar throughout the country.

The warm Australian climate means that people can spend a lot of time outdoors. Barbecues are very popular; in fact, Australians think of the barbecue as their own invention.

8 Cities

The boom city of Perth in Western Australia. When the first American astronauts orbited the earth they could see the lights of Perth twinkling in the empty darkness.

Most Australians live in cities. All the major cities are on the coast, except for Canberra. About two-thirds of the population live in the state or territory capital cities, while fewer than one in seven lives in the country. This makes Australia one of the most **urbanized** countries in the world.

Each of the capital cities has its own character. Sydney is a city of beaches and sun. Australians think of it as an exciting, expensive city, and the one most influenced by the United States. Melbourne, a city of parks and gardens, is quieter and considered very British. Adelaide is a city of churches, but it is also famous for the international arts festival, which is held every two years. Perth is the only major city on the west coast. It is a boom city — discoveries of valuable minerals such as diamonds, nickel, copper and tin have made it a bustling and expanding city. Darwin, in the far north, still has the atmosphere of a frontier town. Brisbane is almost in the tropics, and life there is paced to suit the heat. Hobart, the most southerly city, is quiet and has something of a village atmosphere. Canberra is the capital of Australia and is a city of politicians and public servants.

Most Australian cities developed during the nineteenth century. Most have a city center densely packed with buildings that gives way to spacious suburbs. The suburbs developed as the railroad network spread. Many Australians aim to own their own house and yard, and this has added to the urban sprawl. Australian cities are among the largest in the world in terms of area.

Above *Under the clocks at Flinders Street Railway Station in Melbourne is a popular meeting place.*

Below *Sydney is a mixture of old and new buildings.*

9 Growing up in Australia

Many young Australians live fairly comfortably in the suburbs of the major cities. Houses in Australia are usually single storied with a large yard. Those Australians from non-British cultures often live in extended families — with parents, grandparents and perhaps aunts and uncles. In such a family, older children are responsible for looking after younger brothers and sisters. Some young Australians live in apartments or town houses in the older parts of the cities, while others live on remote sheep or cattle stations. For young people whose parents are separated or divorced, home may be with just one parent.

A young Australian couple gardening outside their home in the suburbs of Sydney.

This Australian Aboriginal family is enjoying a meal at home in Taree, New South Wales.

In urban Aboriginal families, mothers often play an important role. These families may be poorer than many other Australians but they place less emphasis on money and they form a close-knit community and help each other out in times of need. Aborigines believe family duties and responsibilities to be extremely important no matter how distantly related the relative. In the **outback** some Aborigines follow a traditional lifestyle, depending in part on what they can gather for food.

Most Australian teenagers have their own room, often decorated with posters of their favorite pop groups. Younger children usually share a room and perhaps decorate it with pictures of animals or sports heroes. Like young people all over the world, young Australians enjoy sports, and after school many go to train for a local or school team. Cricket, soccer, rugby and Australian Rules football are among the popular Australian sports. Free time at home may be spent playing, reading, listening to music or watching television. On some nights of the week there may be special activities to attend such as scouting or classes to learn the traditional dances and music of their own **ethnic** groups.

The weekend is a time to relax. Many children play for their teams on Saturday morning, and on winter afternoons it is popular to go to a professional sports event. Sunday for some young Australians is the day to go to church. For others it is the day to go to the beach, if the weather is fine.

Left Australian teenagers, like teenagers all over the world, like to decorate their bedrooms with posters.

Opposite This Australian girl is dressed in the traditional Polish costume of her ancestors during a festival in Parramatta Park, Sydney.

Below Australian boys and girls taking a well-earned break during a baseball game.

10 Education

In Australia children must start going to school by the age of six. Most children go to state elementary schools, which are run by the government of the state in which they live, but some children go to private schools. Most of the private schools are run by churches.

The elementary school day usually begins at about 9:00 a.m. with a morning assembly of the whole school followed by classes. In the middle of the morning there is a short break called playlunch. Then, the children go back to classes until lunchtime. The school day finishes at about 3:30 p.m.

Australians must begin school at the age of six and may not leave until they are at least fifteen.

At the end of year six, students leave elementary school and go to secondary school — either a high school or a technical school. Children must go to school until the age of fifteen. Many subjects, such as English, social studies and science, that were taught in elementary school, are also taught in secondary school, along with other subjects such as foreign languages and chemistry. The final year at school is year twelve, although many students have already left by this time.

Above An elementary school teacher instructs her class at a school in Melbourne.

Many students, such as those who live on outback cattle stations, live a long way from the nearest school. There are special schools to teach these children, one of which is the "School of the Air." This school is conducted over the two-way radios that people in the outback use to communicate from one station to the next.

Most Aborigine children attend the same schools as other Australians, though in some areas there are special programs that recognize their different cultural background.

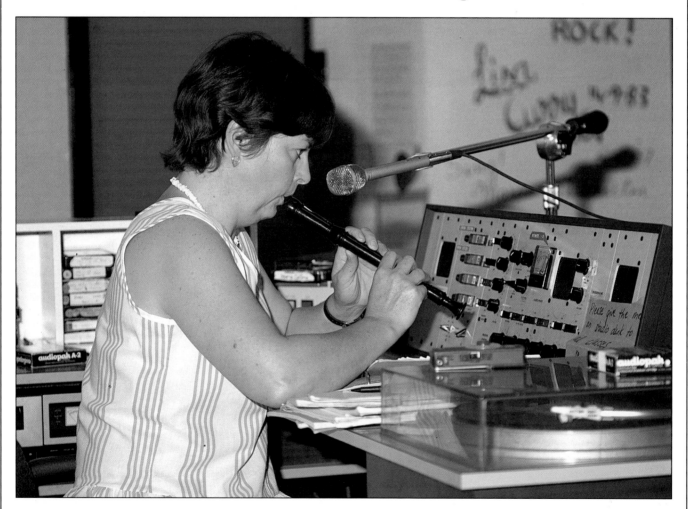

Young Australians who live in remote outback areas are given lessons over the radio by teachers who work for the "School of the Air."

Shopping and food

On almost every street corner in Australian cities there is a corner store, which Australians call a milk bar. It sells all sorts of food and household goods from milk to liquid detergent. Small country towns have a general store, which sells an even greater range of goods, including such items as sheep dip and barbed wire, which are useful in the country. In most suburbs and in many country towns there are now supermarkets where most people do their shopping. Many supermarkets are part of a large chain. Supermarkets are convenient, though the goods are much cheaper at milk bars.

Right Corner milk bars are extremely popular.

Below In the suburbs and rural areas, small stores provide a useful service.

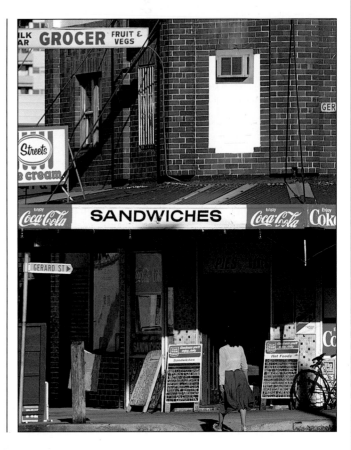

Until World War II, Australian cooking was generally plain and British. Main meals usually consisted of meat — often roasted — and potatoes and vegetables — often boiled. As people from many different countries have come to live in Australia since the war, cooking and tastes have changed. A greater range of foodstuffs has become available in the stores. Many immigrants have set up their own specialty food shops that sell food shipped in from their home countries. Australians have been introduced to salami from Italy, black olives from Greece and sauerkraut from Germany. Many ethnic restaurants have opened, and Australians are now more willing to try different flavors, foods and dishes, and to eat out more often. The wine industry has expanded and Australia now produces many fine wines. These trends have continued as people still come to Australia from all over the world.

Most cities have central business districts where there are large department stores, although people generally prefer to do most of their shopping nearer the home. The cities also have markets where people can buy fresh fruit and other produce from market stalls. There are many stores that sell foods for particular ethnic groups — for example, Asian supermarkets and Italian delicatessens.

Above Australia's coins and dollar notes. The Australian dollar is divided into 100 cents.

Right A sidewalk café selling Italian food in Cairns, North Queensland. Many Italian immigrants came to Cairns as sugarcane cutters and stayed to become farmers and develop businesses.

12 Sports and leisure

Most Australians have a passion for sports — in fact the people Australians admire most are usually sports personalities. The warm climate means they can spend a lot of time outdoors taking part in sports, and there is a lot of space for recreational activities. Televised sports are also popular.

In the summer the major team sport is cricket. Many people will go to watch the English-Australian championship match or watch it on television. There are also local and interstate competitions. Australians are known internationally as tennis players, and the Australian Open is the fourth of the Grand Slam Tournaments. Pat Cash is among the many Australian tennis superstars who have won at Wimbledon.

The beach plays an important part in Australian life in summer. People go sailing, surfing, swimming, windsurfing or just laze in the sun. Australians have always performed very successfully in international swimming competitions. Golf is also a widely played game, even in winter. Winter is also the ski season, and both downhill and cross-country skiing are popular.

The most popular team sport in winter is "football," which is not the same as American football. Several different football games are played in Australia — rugby, soccer and Australian Rules. Australian Rules football is unique to Australia. It first began in the nineteenth century in Melbourne, where

Above *Young Australians enjoying a game of cricket in Alice Springs, Northern Territory.*

Below *Australian Rules football game between Carlton and North Melbourne.*

it continues to be followed fanatically. It is also played in Tasmania and many other parts of Australia. Rugby is one of the favorites in New South Wales and Queensland, and both states have major leagues. Soccer is played all over Australia.

Other team sports played in Australia are basketball, hockey and netball. More people play netball than any other sport. However, of the recreations, fishing is enjoyed by more people than any other.

Windsurfing is an extremely popular sport in Australia. Australians believe that their waves, along with Hawaii's, are the biggest, most dangerous and best surfing waves in the world.

13 Religions, festivals, holidays

Australians follow many different religions. There are Muslims, Hindus, Christians, Sikhs and Jews as well as Buddhists. The religion that has the largest number of followers is Christianity.

Most of the holidays celebrated in Australia are Christian holidays. The most notable holidays are Christmas and Easter. These fall in the winter in Europe and North America. In the Southern Hemisphere, however, December comes in the summer, and many Australians finish their Christmas Day at the beach, swimming or sailing.

Right There are about 80,000 Muslims in Australia. This Islamic mosque is in Canberra.

Below Christmas dinner of roast turkey and plum pudding can be eaten outdoors, as December 25 is the middle of the Australian summer.

Australia celebrated its Bicentennial — 200 years since the first European settlement — on January 26, 1988. Ships sailed into Darling Harbor, Sydney, in memory of the First Fleet of 1788.

The Aborigines' religions involve the worship of their ancestors, of the land and of the spirits that inhabit it. Traditional Aborigines do not see themselves as separate from the land. They do not own it, they belong to it.

There are other Australian holidays that do not have a religious significance. Australia Day falls on January 26 and marks the day Captain Arthur Phillip of the First Fleet began the European settlement of Australia by formally taking possession of Eastern Australia for Britain. The Melbourne Cup is Australia's foremost horse race, and the city of Melbourne takes the day off to celebrate. Perhaps the holiday that is most important to Australians is ANZAC Day, when the thousands of men who died at Gallipoli in Turkey during World War I (1914-18) — Australia's first significant loss at war — are remembered. In Alice Springs a "boat race," the "Henley on Todd," is run each year, on a dry riverbed. The crews run the race carrying their boats.

Culture and the arts

Members of the Sydney Symphony Orchestra giving a public performance.

The first painters who came to Australia from Europe had great difficulty when they tried to paint the Australian landscape. It was so strange and unfamiliar, yet their paintings made it look like a European landscape. The trees were especially difficult to paint. It was not until the late nineteenth century that the Heidelberg School of painters managed to paint the Australian landscape successfully. Australian painters have always struggled to come to terms with their country's unique landscape. This can be seen in the works of Sir Sydney Nolan.

Many people all over the world know Australia from its movies. The first feature movie in the world was made in Australia, but the industry did not really begin to develop until the 1970s. Now its films are known internationally — *Gallipoli* and *Crocodile Dundee* are examples. Australian soap operas such as one called "Neighbors" are also popular in Britain as well as Australia.

Some of the movies and television series are based on works of Australian literature, such as *My Brilliant Career* by Miles Franklin. Soon after their arrival, European settlers wrote of their new country and their writings began to take on an Australian flavor. As Australia developed so did its literature. In 1975 Patrick White, perhaps Australia's best-known contemporary writer, won the **Nobel Prize** for literature.

Music, from popular to classical, ballet, opera and theater have a strong tradition in Australia, as do other major art forms such as sculpture.

Aborigines have a rich culture, and their art is finally beginning to receive the recognition it deserves. The traditional poems, songs, myths and legends are very beautiful. Many Aborigines, such as the poet Kath Walker, are today extending and enriching Aboriginal culture with their own poems and other works of art.

Above Paul Hogan, the Australian actor, writer and comedian.

Right Woman and Billabong — a painting by the famous Australian painter Sidney Nolan.

15 AUSTRALIA
Farming and fishing

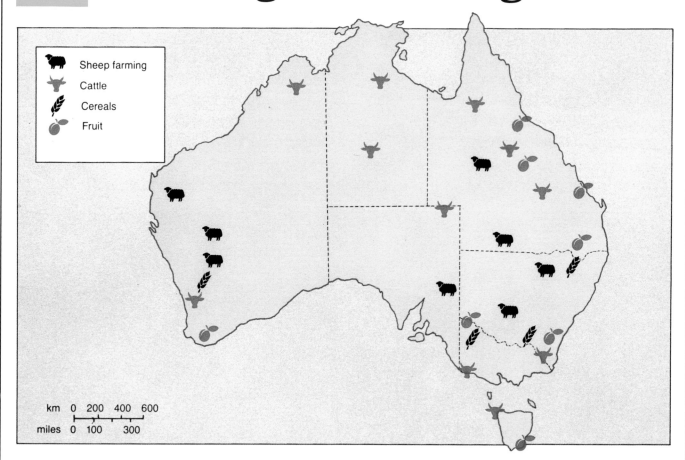

Sheep farming
Cattle
Cereals
Fruit

km   0   200   400   600
miles   0   100   300

In the past, farming was by far the most important industry in Australia. It remains so today, though its importance has fallen somewhat with the rise of manufacturing and mining. Farming still produces one-third of Australia's **export** income, more than either manufacturing or mining. The three largest agricultural industries are wool, beef and wheat.

It is said that Australia "rode on the sheep's back" — it was wool that produced much of the country's early wealth. Australia is still the world's largest exporter of wool. Australians sell their wool to many different countries.

With the development of refrigeration in the late nineteenth century, meat from sheep and cattle could be exported. Since the 1960s an export trade in live sheep with the Middle East has also developed.

Some of the farms, called "stations" in Australia, are very large — larger than an American county — especially in the north and west. Australian cattle are free-range or grass-fed cattle. They graze in grass paddocks rather than being fed grain in sheds. The United States is the major Australian overseas customer, although beef is also sold to Japan and to many other countries.

Many different kinds of fruit are grown in Australia, from bananas and pineapples in tropical Queensland to apples in temperate Tasmania. In the warmer, drier areas inland, citrus trees, including oranges and lemons, are grown under irrigation. Much fruit is exported, either fresh or canned. Important customers include Europe, Britain, Canada and Japan.

Wheat is grown in all states of Australia, except Tasmania, and most of it is exported. The largest customers are China, Egypt, the Soviet Union and Japan. Most wheat farms are run by an owner-farmer and are highly mechanized.

There are many other agricultural products, such as sugar, which is grown in Queensland, that make an important contribution to the Australian economy. Like much else in Australia, farming has expanded since the end of World War II. Wine is now also a major industry, and products such as rice and tobacco are grown.

As Australia has a long coastline, fishing is another important industry. Tuna and salmon are canned, while other fish, such as mullet, whiting and snapper, are caught for the table.

Above Rounding up cattle at a station in Hunter Valley, New South Wales.

Left Sugarcane used to be cut by hand using machetes. Now huge and expensive machines are used.

16 Manufacturing and mining

Above Operating a blast furnace at a steelworks in Newcastle on the New South Wales coast.

Since the turn of the century, manufacturing has played an important role in the Australian economy. Before 1900 most goods were imported (bought from other countries). Manufacturing was boosted by the First and Second World Wars because shipping was reduced and it was difficult to import goods. The growth in manufacturing has been dramatic since the end of World War II. Manufacturing now employs over a million people and it contributes about one-fifth of exports. Industries range from engineering to oil refining and from plastic to paper.

Main exports:	Coal, wool, wheat, iron ore, copper, bauxite, opal, nickel, zinc, uranium, gold, beef, manganese, lead, mineral sands.
Main imports:	Road vehicles, petroleum and petroleum products, office machinery (including computers), industrial machinery, electrical equipment.

Since the discovery of the first commercial oilfield at Moonie in Queensland in 1961, Australian production of oil and its refined products has grown rapidly. There are now a number of commercial fields both offshore, for example in Bass Strait, and on land, for example in the Amadeus Basin in the Northern Territory.

Historically, mining has been important in Australia. The goldrushes of the nineteenth century made the population and economy of Australia grow rapidly. In the 1960s mining again boomed, especially in the north and the west, but this time all sorts of minerals, from nickel to iron ore, were mined.

Above *Aboriginals campaigning against the destruction of their land by mining companies.*

Below *Mining iron ore at Goldsworthy, Western Australia.*

Mining is an important part of the Australian economy. Australia is among the largest exporters of coal in the world and also of bauxite. It is the second largest exporter of iron ore. It is a major producer of such minerals and metals as gold, nickel, copper, manganese, uranium, lead, zinc and mineral sands. Even diamonds are mined in Australia. Japan is a major customer for Australia's resources, and China is becoming increasingly important.

There is sometimes conflict between mining companies on one side and conservationists and Aborigines on the other. Many new discoveries are on Aboriginal land. Some Aborigines and conservationists feel that mines can destroy the history of the land and damage the land itself.

17 Transportation

Australia is a vast country whose population is scattered in pockets around its rim. Perth is as far from Adelaide as San Francisco is from Memphis, Tennessee. This means transportation is difficult, costly and very important.

Most of the goods transported within the country are carried by trucks. Large trucks, called semitrailers, are constantly criss-crossing the country. There is a large road network to carry the trucks, though the roads can be rough, especially in the outback. To carry cattle in the outback a series of trailers are often linked together behind a truck to form a road train.

Railroads also cross the great distances. The Indian-Pacific service from Sydney to Perth via Adelaide covers a distance of 4,348 km (2,700 mi). Besides carrying people, the railroads transport large amounts of minerals, petroleum products and grain. Before 1901, the colonies had no consistent railroad gauge (the gauge is the distance between the rails). Therefore, you had to change trains at the borders. Since the formation of the Commonwealth of Australia, efforts have been made to create a railroad that can serve the whole country.

Above Passengers leaving an Ansett Airlines Boeing 767 in Alice Springs.

Right Camels were first brought to Australia in 1860. Today, thousands still roam the outback, though many carry on their task as "ships of the desert," transporting people across the dry plains.

Australians were among the first to use airplanes for everyday overland transportation. Planes are ideal where the country is rough and roads are few, and many outback cattle stations have an airstrip. In the north and west of Australia, the Flying Doctor Service uses airplanes to bring medical attention to the sick and injured in isolated areas and transport serious cases to the hospital.

Ships are also vital to Australia, which is far away from most of the countries with which it trades. Shipping is needed to carry Australia's exports and to transport bulk items such as mineral ores around the coast. As a result, most major Australian cities have developed around a port.

Above *Passengers board the streetcar in St. Kilda Road, Melbourne. Unlike the other major cities, Melbourne still uses streetcars.*

Below *A tough four-wheel drive truck is the ideal form of transportation on the dusty outback roads.*

18 Government

Australia is a parliamentary **democracy**, and it is also a federation of states, like the United States. In 1901 the self-governing British colonies — New South Wales, Victoria, Tasmania, South Australia, Western Australia and Queensland — joined as states to form the Commonwealth of Australia.

Australia has a federal government plus six separate state governments, one for each of the six states. The federal government is responsible for major things like defense, income tax, immigration and social security. Each state government is responsible for things concerning the particular state, like roads, libraries and housing. All the governments are based on the British and North American systems with an upper and lower house. The lower house, the House of Representatives, is modeled on the British House of Commons. The upper house, the Senate, is modeled on the United States Senate. It was created to represent the interests of the states, and each state has an equal number of **senators**.

A policewoman adjusts a child's helmet so he can ride his bicycle safely.

Above Parliament House in Canberra. In the background is the new Parliament House, opened in 1988.

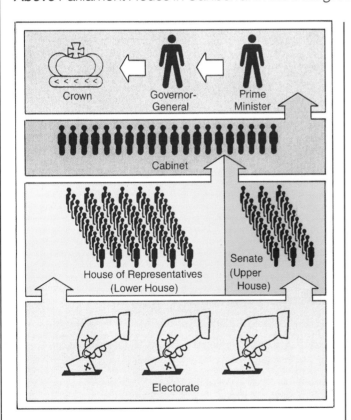

The structure of the Australian government.

There are two main political parties — the Australian Labour Party and the Liberal Party. The political party that has a majority of members in the lower house forms the government, and the prime minister must also be a member of the lower house. It is law that all Australians who are over eighteen years of age must vote.

Queen Elizabeth II is also the queen of Australia. In Australia she is represented by the **Governor-General** and by a governor in each state. Australia is a member of the **British Commonwealth**.

The Australian legal system is based on the British legal system. Each state has its own courts and police force, and there are also courts and a police force at the national level.

19 Facing the future

As in other countries, the economy is a major issue in Australia. Australia is still a prosperous country but it has high levels of unemployment and large foreign debt. Australia was once called "The Lucky Country" in the title of a book. Although it is still "lucky," there is a feeling that the easy days are over and there is a need to work harder and more efficiently.

Race is an issue, though it is unlikely that there will be race riots like those in the United States or Britain. Although Aborigines form a small part of the population, their problems loom large in the public mind. The manner in which their land was taken from them still remains an issue.

Among Australia's many overseas aid projects is this Pasture and Livestock Project in Yunnan, China. The project began in 1983 and to date Australia has spent 5.6 million dollars on it.

One of the great achievements of modern Australia is the way the large number of immigrants — about one-fifth of the population — who have arrived since the end of World War II have settled into the community with so little friction. The number of Asian immigrants is increasing, and many people believe that Australia's population needs to be expanded even further for the economy to be successful.

This raises the issue of Australia's relations with Asia. Australia follows a

Western lifestyle but is situated at the foot of Asia, far from countries with a similar lifestyle. As its links with Britain have weakened, especially after Britain's entry into the **EEC** (European Economic Community), Australia has sought new links and new markets. Many of these are in Asia. In particular Japanese trade links, and also Japan's investments in Australia, are growing. Australia is being bound more tightly into the Asian world.

Below Protesters campaigning for an Australian republic.

Above It is popular for Japanese tourists to come to Australia to get married and honeymoon.

Glossary

Aborigines The original inhabitants of a country. Today, this name also applies to the descendants of the Australian Aborigines.

Alpine Used to describe the climate or plants that are found on high mountains, above the limit for tree growth.

Archaeologists Scientists who study ancient peoples and their remains, especially by finding places where the people used to live.

British Commonwealth A voluntary association of countries that are, or have at some time been, ruled by Britain.

Bush ("the bush") A large uncleared area of land, usually covered with low trees or shrubs.

Colony A settlement of people in a new land, which is ruled by the government of the country they came from.

Conservation Protection of plants and wildlife from the effects of, for example, agricultural and industrial development.

Continent One of the divisions of the earth's land surface. The divisions are Europe, Africa, North and South America, Asia, Australia and Antarctica.

Democracy A political system in which the government is elected by the people.

EEC A group of twelve West European countries (including Britain) who joined together to establish free trade.

Equator An imaginary line making a circle around the earth, halfway between the North and South Poles.

Ethnic Relating to a particular culture.

Eucalyptus Large Australian evergreen tree valued for its oil, gum and timber.

Evolved Developed very gradually.

Export To sell goods to a foreign country.

Extinct No longer existing.

Federation A group of states or nations.

Governor-General The Queen's representative in a particular country.

Habitat The place where a plant or animal lives or grows.

Hardwoods Trees such as oak, beech and ash that have hard wood and are slow growing.

Immigrants People who come to live in a new country.

Mountain building The creation of mountain chains as the massive plates that form the earth's crust push against one another.

Nobel Prize A prize that is awarded every year to people who make outstanding contributions to chemistry, physics, medicine, literature, economics and peace.

Outback The remote inland districts of Australia.

Plateau A broad, level piece of land.

Rain forest A dense forest found in tropical areas of heavy rainfall.

Refugee A person who seeks shelter in another country.

Savannah Open grassland that usually has scattered bushes or trees.

Senator A member of the Senate.

Southern Hemisphere The half of the earth that lies south of the equator.

Stockman In Australia, the man in charge of livestock such as sheep or cattle; also the owner of livestock.

Suburbs Housing areas on the edge of a city.

Temperate Mild in temperature. The temperate areas of the world have a mild climate with neither extremely hot nor extremely cold weather. In the Southern Hemisphere, the temperate regions are between the Tropic of Capricorn and the Antarctic Circle.

Tropics The countries that experience very hot weather. They are found between the Tropic of Capricorn and the Tropic of Cancer — two imaginary lines that are at equal distances north and south of the equator.

Urbanized Greatly influenced by towns and cities; citified.

Wattles Australian acacia trees that have spikes of small, brightly colored flowers.

Books to read

Arnold, Caroline. *Australia Today.* Franklin Watts, 1987

Australia. Time-Life Publications, 1985

Browne, Rollo. *An Aboriginal Family.* Lerner Publications, 1985

Ellis, Rennie. *We Live in Australia.* Bookwright Press, 1983

Gunner, Emily. *A Family in Australia.* Bookwright Press, 1985

Luling, Virginia. *Aborigines.* Silver, Burdett and Ginn, 1979

Lye, Keith. *Asia and Australasia.* Gloucester Press, 1987

Pepper, Susan. *Passport to Australia.* Franklin Watts, 1987

Rau, Margaret. *Red Earth, Blue Sky: The Australian Outback.* Crowell Jr. Books, 1981

Truby, David. *Take a Trip to Australia.* Franklin Watts, 1981

Picture acknowledgments

All photographs were taken by David Bowden with the exception of the following: BBC Hulton Picture Library 15; Bridgeman Art Library 35 (bottom); Bruce Coleman *frontispiece*, 11 (bottom right), 12 (top), 24; Mary Evans Picture Library 14; Christine Osborne 5 (top), 13, 21 (bottom), 23; Topham 35 (middle); Wayland Picture Library 7 (top), 27 (top), 28 (bottom), 39 (bottom), 41 (top); ZEFA 5 (bottom), 20.

Index